BARBED
L·Y·R·E·S

BARBED LYRES

CANADIAN VENOMOUS VERSE

KEY PORTER BOOKS

Canadian Cataloguing in Publication Data

Main entry under title:

Barbed lyres

ISBN 1-55013-252-0

1. Verse satire, Canadian (English).° 2. Canadian
poetry (English) - 20th century.° I. Atwood,
Margaret, 1939-

PS8287.S3B37 1990   C811'.0708054   C90-093717-3
PR9195.85.S3B37 1990

Key Porter Books Limited
70 The Esplanade
Toronto, Ontario
Canada M5E 1R2

Typesetting: Images 'N Type Ltd.

∞ Printed on acid-free paper
Printed and bound in Canada

90 91 92 93 94 95 6 5 4 3 2 1

CONTENTS

Barbed Lyres is, among other things, a tribute to a tradition; the tradition of wittily phrased, morally indignant dissent. Many cultures have practised satiric verse, the Romans and the Scots prominent among them, and in this country the custom of lambasting your enemies by poem goes back a long way — to the scornful rants of Alex McLachlan and the versified curses of Alex Glendinning, through Robert Service and P.G. Hiebert, and thence to Louis Dudek, Irving Layton, Milton Acorn, A.M. Klein and many others.

In 1957, the year I graduated from high school, F.R. Scott and A.J.M. Smith published a book called *The Blasted Pine: An Anthology of Satire, Invective and Disrespectful Verse*. I obtained a copy, Lord knows how. I read it and reread it, glad in that distant and somewhat culturally blank period to be able to read something, indeed anything at all, that acknowledged the country I was living in. The acknowledgment was more like a kick in the pants than a kiss, but it was the opinion of the editors, back in the sleepwalking late fifties, that too much somnolent kissing had gone on of late and that a kick in the pants might be bracing. Although some of the vitriol-spattered objects of these unwelcome attentions have shrunk with time, it's amazing how on-target a lot of the material still is today.

Canadians are often characterized as being overburdened with bland nice-niceness, which is thought to deprive them of edge. Well, not from where I stand! In almost any form you can name, the spirit of satire — dedicated to the tearing of strips off sacred cows, or off any old cow you can get your jackknife into — to the "long war of wit against complacency," as the second edition of *The Blasted Pine* put it — is alive and flourishing. Political cartooning has a number of expert and devastating practitioners in this country; there are at least three funny, mean radio shows, including "The Royal Canadian Air Farce"; satirical songwriters produce apace; theatre regularly goes for the jugular; SCTV had its origins here. No film producer wants to open a movie in Toronto, such is its reputation for eye-gouging. Everything has its flip side, and the flip side of Canadian niceness is bloody-mindedness.

In addition to being a tribute, *Barbed Lyres* is two things: a book and a contest. The contest was sponsored by *This Magazine*, a monthly journal long dedicated to social, political and cultural commentary of a (how shall we say) unmild character. The truth is that in this age of diminishing grants the editors found themselves running short of cash; forced to practise the entrepreneurial self-help advocated by the present government, they decided to raise the needed funds by doing what they do well. (The best defense is offensiveness?) If the said government comes in for a few whacks, it is, after all, only poetic justice.

For the contest, entrants were asked to confine themselves to twenty lines, but were otherwise unlimited: that is, any target was to be considered fair game. The number and quality of the entries were both high, and the judges had a difficult task. There were three judges. The first was Nancy White, regular contributor to CBC's "Sunday Morning" and the author of many excruciatingly accurate songs puncturing topical balloons or delineating the national character. I'll always remember her line about Canadian women, who, when asked if they would like some sex, say "Only if you're having some yourself." The second was Allan Fotheringham, "Doctor Foth" of the back page of *Maclean's* magazine, lambaster of political hypocrisies and social absurdities. The third was *moi*. Don't ask why.

In reading the entries, the judges were looking for manifestations of the satiric spirit: that is, there had to be a target. But mere spitballs and rotten eggs, or mere whining, were not enough: the poem also had to be funny. (This is of course a subjective quality. We tended to go by the shriek-and-snort criterion: if any of the three judges shrieked or snorted during their silent reading, the entry was read out loud to see if the other two would shriek and snort as well.) In addition to that, and not unrelated to it, we were looking for a certain wit, an elegance of expression. If the poem purported to be in metre, it had to scan, more or less. That sort of thing. We tried not to let our own biases, political or otherwise, interfere with our judgement: we were looking for the best-written poems, not the best reinforcements of our own party lines. (Incidentally, the number of entries that rhymed "Meech" with "screech" did lead us to hope that the next time the government holds a national event, it will choose a location whose name allows for a larger variety of rhymes. This is an important consideration too often overlooked by bureaucrats.)

There was general agreement on the top three winners. Tom Denholm's "The Anchor With No Coverage," a beautiful, light-hearted parody of Tennyson on the theme of Peter Mansbridge's head, had a high snort-and-shriek quotient, as did Denis Woolling's and Glen Stone's "Bum Rap," in memory of a famous caress. Brian Davis's "Biz Miz, As Usual" gets the knife in both pointedly and with elegance. Among the next twelve front-runners, there's a welcome variety of both subject and style. Ms. Gerry MacIntosh's "Angleau" is appropriate and well-performed. (By the way, it was noteworthy to us that entries by men far outnumbered those by women. I offer no theory as to the reason, since to suggest that women are as yet less willing than men to be nasty in verse might bring down several different kinds of wrath upon my head.) Terrence Keough's "Mac Bush" is in the excoriating mode of Dryden; and what could be more apropos than Bill Wilson's "Poo River"? But read on. There is much within to delight the soul and sharpen the fang.

Barbed Lyres, the book, contains — of course — the winners of the contest as well as many other poems, and excerpts from poems, selected by the editors both for deadly aim and panache. It also contains twenty-four "invitationals" — poems by professionals or those of high profile, who were invited to submit, not as contest entrants, but just for the fun of it. Robertson Davies shreds — eek! — charities who send you more than one begging letter, Dave Barrett squashes a political opponent, Charles Pachter takes on Canada Post for pirating his painted flag image for their stamp, Richard Hatfield takes aim at pollsters, Pierre Berton does the definitive sentimental Canadian "lake" poem — guess which lake — and many more.

All in all, the response, both to contest and to book, was generous and encouraging. It seems we can still laugh at ourselves, and to some purpose. Satire is by nature subversive — of established opinions, if not of established order — and takes as its point of departure a moral stance: if you have no idea of what you think is right, how can you make fun of a thing for being wrong? As *The Blasted Pine* put it so long ago, "All satire . . . seizes the right of self-assertion. It takes sides, speaks out, and enters actively into social, political, or moral engagements. It is a form of action . . . ."

There's the National Dream, and then there are the National Nightmares. *Barbed Lyres* is about the latter. Nothing takes the national temperature more accurately than a dip into satire. Laugh till you cry.

MARGARET ATWOOD

The Anchor With No Coverage

On either side his temples lie
Long hanks you'd see on any guy;
But lo! A barren space I spy,
Above the glint of steel blue eye,
        The dome of Peter Mansbridge.
Viewers whiten, sound men quiver,
Little producers cringe and shiver;
Will their man remain forever
        The anchor with no coverage?

And what will Wendy Mesley say?
Her hubby balder by the day;
Too late to find a nice toupee.
Oh, well! Her job's safe anyway
        As wife of Peter Mansbridge.
Another day, another strand
Comes off his head on comb or hand.
But still he's loved in all the land,
        The anchor with no coverage.

TOM DENHOLM
OTTAWA

Bum Rap

He is gone, but he's far from forgotten,
For he left many imprints behind.
His hand, it was always extended
For a pat of the jocular kind.
He was ever the locker room kidder,
As he aimed that big paw from the rear,
And at times, you will still see them flinching,
Even though he is no longer here.

So, let's visit the table at Winston's,
And assure him that we still care.
It's a way to keep track of his meathooks,
Assuming he still hangs out there.
But wherever he is, let's not lose him,
Or we'll never be safe from the threat.
There are those who will swear on the Bible
That their buns are still quivering yet.

Yes, I'm getting behind John Turner, again.
It's the only safe place you can be.
I'm getting behind John Turner, again.
So Turner can't get behind me.

GLEN STONE AND DENIS WOOLLINGS
TORONTO

THIRD PRIZE

Biz Miz, As Usual

Though slow, loath to push away the table,
How the rich all rush in mink and sable
To see, securely sunk in red velour,
The bloody insurrection of the poor.
Rapt, they will watch the wretched writhe and roar,
Then stand and clap and cry for more and more.
For them all revolutions are a hit
If sumptuously staged beyond a pit.
The rags tear at their hearts, they feel the pain.
(Real beggars they have shunned — and will again.)
For them that's art's mystery, its magic:
Even their most maudlin thoughts seem tragic.
And so they go and gladly pay to see
What all around them is on view for free.

BRIAN DAVIS
TORONTO

Angleau

The language of 'belles lettres' is so uncouth —
I am too chic, I have too much panache
To speak a single word of it, forsooth!

I have a rendezvous at the ballet
Tonight, to see the famous pas-de-deux:
(A chance to wear my brand new gold lamé)...

Although, the écru peau-de-soie is nice,
(Especially with the little chiffon scarf) —
But No... I have already worn that twice.

My fiancé will call in his Renault,
(Complete with corsage, and with boutonnière)
And then, with great élan, away we'll go.

A theatre-party afterwards, perhaps?
Champagne and petits-fours at Chez Étienne,
With café noir for me, a schnapps for him.

Later, with nonchalance and savoir-faire,
(Consenting adults, both, you may be sure)
We'll end the evening at his pied-à-terre.

I state my case... howe'er the chips may fall,
That English is the language of us all.

GERRY MacINTOSH
VICTORIA

Chinocchio

To unite his torn country, Gepetto
Carved a marionette allegretto.
He formed his chin great,
To help him orate,
Lest his speeches be made in falsetto.

Chinocchio said he had a vision;
He'd sew up his country's incision.
But he couldn't afford
E'en the cost of a cord;
"He's a leech," people laughed in derision.

Though reluctant to share future glories,
The coy puppet signed up with the Tories.
But in speech after speech
People still called him "leech,"
And his chin grew with each of his stories.

The two factions at last said, "We're bored;
You said you'd sew up the discord."
But Chinoke came unstrung,
So the folks this taunt flung:
"No strings? Can't the leech make a cord?"

VICTOR EMERSON
OTTAWA

Football and Hockey Higgledy-Piggledies

I
CFL dynamo
Mister Ralph Sazio
Managed his teams with a
Chair and a whip.

Joining the Boatmen, he
Gave them direction and
Skilled navigation, and
Then he jumped ship.

II
Habitant pugilist
Mister John Ferguson
Fought by convention but
Skated so strange.

Once paraphrasingly
Stated quite proudly he'd
Not met a face he could
Not re-arrange.

NEIL DICKINSON
OTTAWA

Brian the Vth

Act III. Scene I. New France, Before Hull.

[Alarum, etc.]

> Once more into the Meech, dear friends, once more,
> Or fill the lake up with our Tory dead.
> In politics there's nothing so becomes
> A member than to show obedience.
> In times when in the polls our strength is high
> Then lightly wear we all the mantle of
> Authority. But when our fortunes hang
> So much in desperate estate then must
> We all in unison acclaim our cry,
> For Brian, the party and the accord.

TERRY RYAN
HALIFAX

The Ending Was Swell
But the Rest Was Sheer Hell

A cheap package bus tour of Hades
would be painless compared to the eighties.
Thank God we got into the nineties
with our lives and some clean lakes and pine trees.

BOB WAKULICH
MILL BAY, BRITISH COLUMBIA

When Gallup Calls

Watch-wearing workers, impeccably dim,
forthright and digital, pixelboard temperate —
these are the hands on a hundred-odd phones
when the Gallup amphigory weekly begins.

The questions are simple: what's your age? sex?
    and waist size?
Do you go to church often? vote Liberal? or both?
Can you name the ten provinces? Can you name
    all your kids?
How's your mileage? your income? your stocks?
    and your heart?

Do you trust the prime minister? the U.S.? the pope?
Would you take a vacation? an aspirin? your life?
Do you understand Meech Lake? the I Ching? And, oh,
thanks a lot for your time. Don't forget to hang up.

Then the call's over, and soon the flotsam identity,
the Average Canadian, steps out Gallup's doors,
taking the streets in a Frankenstein shuffle,
sporting a fresh set of emperor's clothes

while the sky splits open with a thunder of hooves
and the clarion trumpet-call of heavenly hosts
singing celestial praises to nobody in particular.

CLIVE THOMPSON
TORONTO

The Killer Whale

Killer Whales will, in a trice,
give up the freedom of the ice
to caper in Marineland Parks;
to dive and jump and suchlike larks.

Now, why is it, do you suppose,
that whales desert the Arctic floes?

Beneath the ice, it can be banked on
they're broke and must dine cheap on plankton,
and when the funds get really low
there's bit-part work for Jacques Cousteau.

But in Marinelands, hours are shorter,
a union wage and nice clean water,
all the herrings a whale can scoff
and every other weekend off.
But best of all — a vote would show —
there's no more bloody Jacques Cousteau.

R. MACPHEE
TORONTO

Oh, Canada? Revised Case History

With apologies to Earle Birney

We re-examine the case of the high-school land,
Grown paunchy and suffering from mid-life crisis —
The once nervous laugh now a Rotarian bray,
On the verge of divorce and in psychoanalysis.
His sudden fists have become quite tame,
He's trying to date a Southerner.
His manners have markedly improved abroad
Though he is still afraid of foreigners.
At home his dreams are filled with aquarian terrors,
Nine fish fried, but one still astray.
That one's a cod, wanting respect and recognition,
Nobody's patsy and struggling away.
Who's this appearing for one last reprise?
The flower man who shrugs and says: *"Au fait,*
On the one hand a fish, on the other *un poisson.*
That's the only way to save the day."
To conclude, schizophrenia has become acute,
Our patient's self-image stuck in adolescence.
Still we must ask ourselves whether this is
A case of self-defeat or just planned obsolescence?

STEPHEN M. GRANT
TORONTO

In Praise of the Triple-E Senate

Let's reform the Senate of the Parliament of Canada:
Make it Equal
and Elected and Effective and Everything.
Equal?
Equal means you give mountains and forests and prairie
   hectares
equal representation with people!
One hectare, one vote, eh?
Precisely!
Why not?
The Elected Senator for a million hectares of Alberta
   woodland
could stand up in the Chamber
and say Effectively,
My constituents strongly object to being cut down
and ground up
and flattened out into sheets of paper!
And so the long-suffering earth
would at last have a voice
in the Parliament
that decides her fate,
eh?

ROBERT FISCHER
EDMONTON

Ode to Jean Charest

*A Patriotic Poem in the shape of
the finish of a 100-metre dash
(to the tune of "O Canada")*

Blah blah blah blah
Blah blah blah blah blah blah
Blah blah blah blah
Blah blah blah blah blah blah
Blah blah blah blah
Blah blah blah blah
Blah blah blah blah blah blah
Blah blah blah blah
Blah blah blah blah
Blah blah blah blah blah blah
Blah blah blah blah
Blah blah blah blah
Blah blah blah blah
Blah blah blah blah blah blah
Blah blah blah blah
Blah blah blah blah b-l-a-h b—l—a—h

DAVID HUNT
TORONTO

Mac Bush: A Mock Epic

With apologies to Dryden — John, not Ken

Of continental drift I sing, in sighs
As melancholy as "When Irish Eyes"
The young Mac Bush sang on a sham-rock stage,
The corporation minion of his age.

Poetic justice these grave lines infuse,
Inspired by Minnie and by Mickey Muse!

Then spoke the President: "Of northern swine,
Mul_____, only, is a son of mine;
As Mac Bush he's the likeliest one I see
To manifest to us th'entire piggery.
Others there yearn for independent fates:
Mul_____ longs for these United States."

Then Mac Bush stood, his bum stuck out behind,
Mendacity, as usual, filled his mind;
He said: "Although I love this country much,
It lacks the gentler U.S. business touch;
And guns at hand, and slums, and unsafe streets!"
The crowd cried out with answering oinks and bleats!

And so the bordering tectonic plates
Were welded into indecipherable states.

TERRENCE KEOUGH
OTTAWA

Heartcry of an Over-Solicited Donor

The bleeding haemorrhoid and the fallen womb
The harsh rejection on the Day of Doom
Reward those wretches whose unwearied greed
Clutters my postbox with their wails of need!

Hospitals are falling down
Falling down, falling down;
Children raped all over town,
My wee victim-O!

I know that times are tough and want's a rover;
Oil coats the ducks and the whale swims for cover;
Old Venice sinks, Public Broadcasting quails;
Cancer and AIDS speed under swelling sails.

I've responded through the mail —
Open purse, never fail;
Now I'm sick of being nice —
Bugger all who bill me *twice!*

All those who grin, in answer to my frown,
"It isn't *our* fault; the computer's down."
Deepest damnation, past all hope of Heaven
On those who beg when I've already GIVEN!

ROBERTSON DAVIES
TORONTO

Glowing Tribute

There's this girl I know on the Danforth
who goes to Buffalo to shop
for the bargains on Bill Blass sheets
and with her parents to Polish nights in Orillia where
she says she wouldn't be caught dead if the perogies
weren't to absolutely die.

She takes her vacations in Warsaw almost every year
because she tells me the deals on crystal are
incredible and she can stay cheap with her Aunt Stenya.

It's not like Mary isn't into Canada
she did Banff in '82
and drove all by herself to P.E.I. in '84
where by the way she lucked in
to a fabulous villa timeshare in the Caymans
because thanks to God she had American Express on her.

In the back window of her Beamer with the Blaupunkt
there's one of those Canadian flag stickers
and it glows at night
I mean what do you want from her
it isn't like she was born here.

TRICIA McCALLUM
MARKHAM, ONTARIO

Faust, Part Three

The Devil slithered up the Drive
And sidled to the door.
"Come in!" said Brian smilingly,
"I think we've met before!"

"Come in and sit!" Mulroney said,
Avuncular and kind,
"Now, tell your leader, if you will
What's troubling your mind!"

"It's Faust, you see," the Devil said,
"My tempting made him lax
And meek and mild — I bought his soul —
But now there's this damned TAX!"

Said Brian, condescendingly,
"I tax all things of worth;
Inflation's in the Heavens,
So I'll bring it back to earth."

The Devil smiled! — He did! he smiled!
"Come, tax my souls as well!
A man who taxes books and art
Is welcome down in Hell!"

JOHN GERTRIDGE
WATERLOO, ONTARIO

Grave Consequences

Lay off food containing fat,
Cholesterol's a killer.
Don't eat this and don't eat that,
The cries get ever shriller.

Monosodium glutamate
Packaged foods contaminate.
Coffee's bad and tea is out,
Chocolate, worse without a doubt.

Do not smoke, it's bad for you.
Alcohol is poison too.
Impure sugar, doctored meat;
What the hell is safe to eat?

I followed what the experts said;
Now of hunger I am dead.
And having left this mortal coil
I, in turn, pollute the soil.

JOHN BENSON
VICTORIA

Laurier's Child

At last
a clue to the crime of the century

Newspaper headlines reveal
each day in Canada
three children kidnapped
by a parent

Was it Uncle Sam or Mother Britain
who substituted this undistinguished whelp
for the golden cherub of the twentieth century?

Quick
alert Child Find to the case
cover milk cartons and billboards with
... what face?

WENDY PETERS
TORONTO

24 Sussex Driven

There once was a man from Shawinigan,
Who was out, but aspired to be inigan.
Ce n'est pas difficile, for we all seem to feel
We will never elect The Big Chinigan!

DENIS WOOLLINGS
TORONTO

Saltchuck

Cremation was always his thing
"I don't want to clutter the yard," he'd say
While chucking his beer can into the bush.
"Folks leave such a mess when alive
So just chuck my ashes into the chuck
And say I've gone out with a little chuckle."
Shortly he got his wish when the skidder flipped.
We logged a few acres to make his pyre
And partied all night at his drunken wake.
We floated his ashes out on the tide
But left lots of empties for his monument.

WILLIAM PETERS
VICTORIA

A Love Song for a Cold Canadian

I grow cold... I grow cold...
I shall wear the top of my tuque unrolled.

Shall I leave the past behind? Do I dare to eat the Meech?
Shall I go down south, get some sun on a beach?
I have heard the politicians singing, each to each.

I do not think that they will sing to me.

STUART PETERSON
TORONTO

Poo River

Little drops of water
coming down the pipe,
make a mighty river
mighty overripe.

In that mighty river
fish got mercury.
Give that mighty river
an A in chemistry.

Lot of ducks come down here
looking for to coop;
should have read the menu,
now they're in the soup.

Preacher shoved him under,
hollering, "Repent!"
He did and got a mouthful,
which is how he went.

Gotta be some changes!
How about it, boss?
Your mill upon the river's
no Mill upon the Floss.

BILL WILSON
VANCOUVER

Sunday Report

When J.M. Barrie penned the joys
Of Peter and Wendy and all the Lost Boys
In Neverland, did he foresee
Sunday Report, on CBC TV?
"Our panel," says Peter with a smile
Reminiscent of the ticking crocodile,
"Will look at issues of the day
In a thoroughly objective way.
Here's Wendy, to report on Ottawa's strife —
Oh, did I mention she's my wife? —
And Halton's here, to countervail
My friend Jeff Simpson of the *Globe and Mail.*
Free thinkers, all; it's nice to see
Such a range of opinion on the CBC
I wouldn't exactly call us cronies,
Though we dined last night at Mulroney's.
We're journalists, rid of any bias
As we gather each Sunday on this dais.
Now, who will be the first to advise us
How well the government's meeting its latest crisis?"

ERIKA RITTER
TORONTO

EXCEPTIONAL BISQUE, MILA, COMME D'HABITUDE

Do Not Disturb

It is illegal to bother a walrus in Canada —
except to kill it. "No person shall willfully
disturb a walrus," says a regulation published
in *The Canada Gazette*. But licences are available
to kill the animals. *(news item)*

Ssh! A walrus! Diffident beast,
he's not to be disturbed.
We must respect his inner peace,
the urge to bug him curbed.

We *may* annoy an oyster, or
badger a bear if we must.
But tiptoe 'round *this* carnivore:
a walrus is not to be fussed.

Despite his awesome overbite,
the pinniped may swoon,
if startled on his Arctic site,
or hassled with harpoon.

We're free, of course, to kill the brute.
The licences are there.
What must remain beyond dispute:
as Canadians, we *care*.

ERIC NICOL
VANCOUVER

A Canadian Speaks to God (or Whatever)

The weary Canadian gazed at the sky,
his smile and his spirit gone limp.
"I seem to be stuck in this country, but why?"
Bellowed God, "Cause I put you there, wimp."

JOHN GOODCHILD
TORONTO

Pork Pourri

I cooked this morning morning's mignon,
    kingdom of breakfast's Bacchus, basted back-sliced
    Bacon in his frying
    On the level skillet, underneath him steady heat and lying
Flat there, until hot steel began to sting,
Making eggs tasty! then sizzle, sizzle and sing
    As kettle's steam starts silent, slow and sighing
    Then shrills, fills the air. My mouth, near dying,
Raced for a taste, — the devour of, the gastronomy of the
    thing!

Smoke, salt and savour and fat, oh, spit, crisp, snap, all
    Spatter! AND the grease that leaps at me then in flight
A billion times more scalding, more menacing, O my
    Cholesterol!

    No wonder of it: dark grill makes egg white
White, and pasty omelettes pour, fall
    In blackened pan and rise gold-brown and light.

DAVID FRASER
OTTAWA

Hiawatha's Heritage

By the shores of old Lake Erie
Near the turgid big sea water
Stepping o'er the sludge and garbage
Patient summer children staring
At the grey/brown shining water
On this pleasant summer morning
But the signs go up again now
Seems the lake's not fit for humans
Nasty things are in the water
Too unspeakable to mention
Plenty lakes but none to swim in
Cry the woeful summer children
But it's only half the story
For we cannot drink tap water
Drink from out of plastic bottles
Happy, sparkling mineral water
And the air we breathe polluted
Don we now our rubber gas masks
Summer children now are wondering
Who bequeathed this loony planet?

DOREEN MAKEPEACE
TORONTO

The Love Song of H. Bourassa

'Dare I eat a Meech?'

Let us go then, say goodbye,
While a nation mumbles at our side,
like a polity ravished on conference tables.
Let us go to certain half-deserted retreats,
Those muttering retreats
of restless nights in one night CN Hotels,
and sawdust emotions and games of shells.
Retreats that engage in tedious arguments
of insidious intent.
That lead us to the overwhelming question.
Oh do not say you'll miss it,
We'll haggle, you can visit.

In the rooms the premiers come and go,
and some say "oui" and some say "non".

BROOKS B. TOWER
CALGARY

26

The Love Song of Brian J. Mulroney

A mare usque ad Gananoque

Let us go friend, just you and Bry,
With the country served up like a pie
Ready for carving at some conference table.
Let us go then with our half-baked scroll.

In the backroom the pollsters come and go
Speaking of Jacques Parizeau.

Should I have dared to eat the Meech?
So it wasn't one of my better decisions.
How was I to know it'd need a few revisions?

In the backroom the Tories come and go
Speaking of my odds in Baie Comeau

I have seen the moments of my term run quicker.
I have seen the latest Gallup figure.
I know the polls . . . I know the polls . . .
I shall soon assume a somewhat different role.

P.H. KEEFE
TORONTO

Canadian Culture

Some people hate to write about
Beavers,
And sneer at the lonely cry of the
Loon.
They liken them to the gift shop at
Niagara
Where you buy Japanese plastic
Mounties
While wearing a t-shirt with I Heart
Canada.

I wish those people
Would smack their tails
And disappear.

People who don't like
Beavers
Should go and live in
Miami.

BRIAN STEWART
MISSISSAUGA, ONTARIO

Widow's Pique

Beneath thy feet my man Sam Smith
Who lacked enuf to do it with
And now he lies a full two yarde
And every inch be stiffe and harde.

PATRICIA SMITH
DUNCAN, BRITISH COLUMBIA

The Beckoned Coming

Turning and turning in the widening mire
The premier cannot hear of unity;
Things fall apart; the centre cannot hold;
Mere fractiousness is loosed upon the land,
The gold-rimmed tide is loosed, and everywhere
The ceremony of nationhood is drowned;
The feds lack all conviction, while the banks
Are full of passionate intensity.

Surely some evolution is at hand;
Surely the Beckoned Coming is at hand. The Beckoned
    Coming!
Hardly are those words out when a vast image out of *Wall
    Street Journal*
Troubles my sight: somewhere in the lands of the greenback
A shape with broker body and the head of a man,
A gaze blank and pitiless as a gun, is moving its quick eyes,
While all about it reel shadows of the jobless northern herds.
The darkness drops again; but now I know
That twenty decades of covetous sleep
Were vexed to merger by a rocking cradle,
And what rough beast, its hour come round at last,
Slouches toward Ottawa to be born?

LIONEL D. SMITH
SCARBOROUGH, ONTARIO

Meeching for Everyone

All the pigs are at the trough,
at least Mulroney is:
and lord knows what they'll do to us,
we'd better ask Joe Ghiz.

It's Meeching this and Meeching that,
our P.M.'s strong and true,
he bought the last election, boys,
he'll buy the next one too.

The prairie farms are half foreclosed,
ten thousands wives are grey;
and a hundred thousand Free Trade jobs
to the good ol USA.

It's Meeching this and Meeching that,
and maybe it's the end,
and down in history we'll go,
especially our P.M.

While France gets half our stock of fish,
the US gets the rest;
bank interest it's gone through the roof,
likewise freight rates out west.

It's Meeching this and Meeching that,
while the G.S. Tax destroys
all but the smile of our dear P.M.
and Mila and the boys.

We've lasted near 200 years
since Wolfe from sea to sea,
and politicians come and go,
and dogs survive their fleas.

It's Meeching this and Meeching that,
and kids they must throw rocks,
and dogs must bark and ducks must quack,
and politicians talk.

But say one thing and say it once,
                          but why not say it twice?
— if Canada goes down the drain
because of you, Brian — boy,
leave this land damn quick, little man,
and never show your face for shame,
and never show your face again.

AL PURDY
AMELIASBURGH, ONTARIO

The Foth and Ottawa

Do you think
A Shrink
And
Allan Fotheringham
Together
Could gather
What really is
Bothering 'im?

SEN. ROYCE FRITH
OTTAWA

Ancient Rune

Summer is icumen in;
Lewde bring icèd te!
Swetteth guest and bareth chestë,
When gonne I wud they be
Before they scruth me. Scru me!

Splasheth poole and swingeth racquet,
Smiteth croquet balle my kne.
Buzzeth bar-fleen, rotteth their een,
Scurvier sodds I naver se.
Harde Stilton: scru me, scru me!

Goddamme, they draineth every dram, *éheu!*
So now 'gainst summer's golden hemme
No longer rail I: scru me, scru me!
Instede I hoick up full goode phlegm
And sing I now: scru them, scru them!
Scru them!

BOB ASHFORTH
VICTORIA

Doing the Hoochie-Gucci

Myron Baloney had ordered a pony,
  And wanted the beast shoed by Gucci;
Across the whole land, both the humble and grand
  Near gagged on their Seagram's Crown Hoochie.

Then Johnny Cretonne declared that he, for one,
Considered it flagrantly outré;
"In such a tough time, is it not a damn crime
An animal so to accoutré?"

And Maudlin McAwdry said it was tawdry,
But typical Myron Bay-Streeting;
"My own kids, like yours, have an old hobbyhorse.
With whom is Baloney competing?"

At Gucci itself, they just reached for some pelf;
As they said, "What is there to deplore?
It's just a small horse, and you all know, of course,
That we've shoed some big asses before."

ALAN R. LOMBERG
SAULT STE. MARIE, ONTARIO

The National

O turgid eloquence —
O scrupulous verbatim —
The flagrant foible
Diligently spied.

O stringent reticence —
O pious arrogance
Unflinchingly and
Modestly decried.

Terse, tightly-texted testament
So elegantly dictioned;
Prudently apolitical —
Punctiliously non-fictioned.

Meticulous orthoepy
Frequently fallacious —
Prose made as poetry
Relentlessly gracious.

LAMONT TILDEN
TORONTO

Four Daughters

I raised four daughters all by myself
and nary a one was left on the shelf.

How — do you ask — did that come to be?
It was simply a matter of watching TV.

No lessons required — my girls are all grads
They got their diplomas from watching the ads.

Just use the right toothpaste, cream rinse and shampoo
and the next thing you know, they'll be saying "I do."

JESSICA BURTON
BRAMPTON, ONTARIO

Mornings Eyed

A curious fellow, Pete Gzowstic
Was of practically all things agnostic.
In search of what's certain
He lifted each curtain
With the fearless aplomb of a Fosdick.

BILL ELLIS
WINDSOR, ONTARIO

Except for Laura Secord

(or Famous Women from Canada's Past)

This nation was founded by men,
fought for bled for
divvied up by men who didn't
eat dinner,
change their underwear,
make holes in their socks,
or father children.
We know this is true because
women are not mentioned in
history books, except for
Laura Secord who invented
ice cream with the help
of her cow.
Except for Laura Secord,
women did not come from England
and France, their footfalls
did not stir the forests,
their soup did not boil in
fireplaces, their laundry
never hung from trees,
so their children remember
them only in dreams.

SYLVIA MAULTASH WARSH
WILLOWDALE, ONTARIO

The Youthful Offender

I'm really not bad, I'm a loveable lad,
And you haven't the right to say I'm mad.
If I rape your sister and stab your aunt
You can't do a thing to say I can't
. . . I'm a youthful offender.

I've shaved my head and pierced my ears.
To show my defiance in teen-age years.
I could stomp your son and steal his jacket
Or even run a protection racket,
And there's nothing the law could do but hack it.

My parents say I'm their pride and joy, so
They don't believe their fair-haired boy
Would swarm the malls, graffiti the walls.
Threaten the teacher, smoke pot or do crack
I got 'em well trained. I don't get any flak.

Your Grandma's real lucky, it coulda been worse
That she just broke her hip when I snatched at her purse
I'm so cute, young, and sexy, a hot-blooded sport
So I'll just get probation in Juvenile Court
. . . I'm a youthful offender.

DORIS LETTS
HAMILTON, ONTARIO

The Man With the Big Chin

There was a man whose chin
Was the size of Lake Michigan
He was quite saucy
And his manner bossy
'Cause his brain was as large as a pin.

GRADE 4/6/8 CLASS
FALCON BEACH SCHOOL
FALCON LAKE, MANITOBA

British North America, Vigilant We Are for Thee

This anthem was officially received in the fall of 1941 by Their Britannic Majestics King George VI and Queen Elizabeth through the good offices of Sir Allen Lascelles, the King's Private Secretary and Keeper of the Royal Archives. The anthem was first sung in late October 1941 in the assembly hall of the United Left Labour Zionist Freedom Workers' Temple. The anthem was written by Yakov Yoisher, a pants presser by day — an anthem writer by night. At the time Yoisher wrote this officially-received anthem, the Dominion of Canada was officially anthemless. Yoisher's anthem broke the anthem sound barrier. "Oh Canada" inevitably followed. Larry Zolf found "British North America, Vigilant We Are For Thee" in the basement of the Jewish Public Library in Winnipeg — to the right of the furnace and to the left of the Monty Hall Collection. Mr. Zolf was doing research on Victory Gardens, North Winnipeg, 1939–1945. He still is.

Oh! British North America!
Land of the Brave
And Home of the Free,
We British Canadians are on the ready
Vigilance for Thee.

British is Best
For the trapper, the furrier,
The farmer, and the city scurrier.
Being British Brings out the
Best in all Canadians true.

Be they Montreal Catholic, Toronto Protestant
  Or Winnipeg Jew,
Be they Ontario Orangemen
Or Men in Nova Scotia boats, or Manitoba Ukrainians in
  sheepskin coats.

British is Best
For Canadians sipping their tea cups
Be they Albertans in stirrups
Or French Canadians in maple syrups.

British is Best
For all right-thinking.
As for the rest, let them go on
Stinking
Up the place,
For nothing should ever
Stop the British race,
From always setting
The agenda and the pace.

Rule Britannia,
Britannia rules the Waves.
British Canadians, shall never never
Be slaves.

Oh! British North America!
Land of the Brave
Home of the Free
We British Canadians
Are ever ready
To be Vigilant for Thee.

LARRY ZOLF
TORONTO

The Grave-diggers of Canada

The grave-diggers of Canada seem
Nice Enough.
Some are even among my
Best of Friends.
They shrug their shoulders
and nod their heads
and say they understand my
Point of View.
What, then, explains all their
Glee?

JOHN FRASER
TORONTO

Ode to Canada Post

Upon the issue of the 39-cent flag stamp, which strongly resembled the artist's own flag paintings.

Whose flag this is I think I know,
Although you added clouds, and so
As plagiarists you will be cursed
Since I'm the one who did it first!

CHARLES PACHTER
TORONTO

I'd Run Away With Leonard Cohen

I'd run away with Leonard Cohen
If he ever asked
But he won't

I'm a non-smoker and Leonard Cohen
Seems bent on self-destruction
By nicotine

I'm partial to herringbone tweeds
And lovat green socks on men
He wears black

Except when he wears the blue raincoat
And I bet it's not an Aquascutum
Not the type

I listen to Leonard Cohen on CBC
But don't buy his tapes or CDs
CBC is free

I'd run away with Leonard Cohen
But now he really won't ask.

SALLY DEUTSCHMANN
CANMORE, ALBERTA

The Cancelled *Canadian*

*On cancellation of railway
service to Calgary*

Quo vadis, VIA?

No more on singing rails
by prairie trails
to Calgary.

Quo vadis, VIA?

Craigellachie cries
for the promise
lost to posterity

the last spike
struck in vain

this
is the last
straw.

ROSALEE VAN STELTEN
CALGARY

44

My Rose Bush on Meech Lake

I seek ten buds
uhhh, find only seven

Kermit McKenna spreads
constitutional compost
Big Bubba Bourassa
rejects all cuttings
former gardener Trudeau
uhhh, lacerates leaves
with federalist fingers
Clyde breathes fog
chilling words

Uhhh, my roses wither
all petals curl
their former life
once in my grasp
stains my hands
uhhh, the opinion polls
My rose bush droops
now shapeless, uhhh
indistinct.

MARGOT A. FRENCH
OTTAWA

Without S.I.N.

Winnipeg Willie is a peculiar fellow.
His eyeballs are red and his molars are yellow.
He stays out at night with his wineskin and books.
He lets his hair grow and mucks up his looks.
His body is scraped up and bruised from the fights
or the seizures he has in the fields late at night.

He swaggers and blusters that his dad is God.
He can changed wine to water or multiply cod.
He speaks in strange mutters and rolls back his eyes.
And often is found staring up at the skies.
But perhaps the ruckus that caused all the din
Is Willie's admission to be without S.I.N.

To be without S.I.N. is a limiting quirk.
And this, said poor Willie, is why I don't work.
So he hangs out with hookers and distracted sailors.
And makes the acquaintance of various jailors.
But regardless of vices and misguided love,
it's possible the bum could have come from above.
And the one thing home rule is unable to chin
Is a Winnipeg Willie who's barren of S.I.N.

GLEN BECKER
KELOWNA, BRITISH COLUMBIA

A Neo-Imperialist Lament

What has become of Canada, a nation true and blue,
When Sikhs can join the musical ride, the same as me and
  you?
What has become of Canada, a nation true and blue,
When Native mounties dare to ask to wear their hair down
  too?

What has become of Canada, one language for us all,
When French immersion's in the land, and even in the mall?
What has become of Canada, one language for us all,
When money is spent on French intent, can you believe the
  gall?

What has become of Canada, one religion for us all,
When social clubs and video stores replace the old church
  hall?
What has become of Canada, one religion for us all,
When Muslims, Jews and Tim Buck toos can even have a
  ball?

What has become of Canada, with no planned immigration,
When Africans, Asians, and Latins too spread across the
  nation?
What has become of Canada, with no planned immigration,
Without the privileged class to defend its place and station?

DONALD POWER
THUNDER BAY, ONTARIO

My Earth Friendly Bag

Words for a wrap song

I got my DDT coffee
in my CFC cup
and my saran wrap sandwich
halfway eaten up
in my fossil fuel ferrari
I'm out on the main drag
bringing home the bacon
in an earth friendly bag

I bought a bushel of batteries
and some nitrate potting soil
I'll fix my squeaky pin head
with half a can of motor oil
that I keep with a jar of solvent
and some shiny covered mag
along with my Candu tomatoes
in an earth friendly bag

I got a plastic bottle of water
and some teakwood chopsticks cheap
some stripmined clear cut defoliant spray
and some brown coal to make heat
plus a back-up pack of smokes
and some pills to make me gag
along with my young conservative card
in my earth friendly bag

ROBERT PRIEST
TORONTO

The Ghost of P. Trudeau

To be sung aloud to the tune of
"Ghost Riders in the Sky"

T'was late at night in Ottawa, the leader toiled alone,
Catching up on patronage, networking on the phone;
When all at once his jaw dropped to the desktop down below
Through the media the voice of . . . the Ghost of P. Trudeau.

Scornful Jesuit logic descended in a flood,
Traitor, weakling, swindler — words to chill the blood;
The leader groped for platitudes to praise his policy
What catch phrase could he find to match . . . the just society.

Nowhere to hide, nowhere to go . . .
The Ghost of P. Trudeau.

He hit the redial to Bourassa — the fax machine went beep,
Called his colleague David Peterson — the premier was
asleep;
Trudeau cackled hollow laughter — "O dial from sea to sea
Then hang up and hear the curse of . . . the just society.

Your deficit will hobble you, free trade will drain you dry,
GST will be a failure, Meech Lake won't ratify.
Then the Trudeau apparition disappeared into Quebec
Soon to be replaced by . . . the spectre of Lévesque.

Nowhere to hide, nowhere to go . . .
The Ghost of P. Trudeau.

JOHN GRAY
VANCOUVER

Lottery Numbers Lost

Oh why is it that the *Globe and Mail* doesn't publish the
    winning lottery numbers,
anymore?

They used to, you know, and it did make a lot of sense!

I won't ever be able to afford all the expensive stuff they
    advertise
unless I win the big one!

Doesn't the *Globe* want me to discover through them
that I have won a mil' (or two or ten)?

Would they rather I find out through the *Sun*
and be forced to sneak a peek at the Sunshine Girl?

or the *Star*
(and have their editorial writers make me feel guilty about
    being rich)?

It just seems sorta' weird that they won't print those winning
numbers
when every day
they run the closing quotations
for the Vancouver Stock Exchange.

WAYNE GIBSON
ETOBICOKE, ONTARIO

Horizontal Cleavages

On a visit to Parliament Hill
one summer
my purse fell open
leaving my personality strewn
across the floor
Pardon me, I thought
to the other tourists
as I groped for
fragments of myself,
my cleavage is showing

LINDA GYULAI
MONTREAL

My Lake

Memories come flocking back
Like errant sheep,
Memories seeded before real memory began;
Memories of a phantom lake, moonstruck,
And I in my crib, hard by the window,
Peeping through half-open shutters
Gurgling and cooing at the parental slap
Of the persistent waves caressing the shore.

Memories of childhood,
Of skinny-dipping in the cove beyond the cottage,
White buttocks flashing wetly in the sunlight.

51

(We marvel at the rough, male kiss of the sand
while filching quick, embarrassed glances at each other's
loins.)

Memories of youth . . .
I, still a stripling,
Groping for Mavis in the canoe.
The mysterious globe of the moon
Illuminating her own twin globes,
Whiter than the moon herself —
I see them now,
Reflected in the shivering waters of the lake,
And I yearn for them still.
Ah, Mavis! After you came to me
I thought the lake itself —
My lake! — had moved beneath us
Before the canoe capsized.

My lake! the memory of its wetness
(For this lake was ever wet)
Soothed my fever in those distant climes
When I, ever the wanderer,
Roamed far from its shores,
Hunting the elusive *thork*
In the bush country of the *Graal,*
Or seeking the missing *khazibe* people
That luckless tribe whose members
They do say still cling to tenuous life
In the gnarled Mountains of the Lost.

The years have not been kind;
My step falters, my sight is blurred.
Only the lake endures,
I tell myself,
When, home at last,
I make one final pilgrimage to its shores.

Yet somehow it eludes me, my beautiful lake.
Why does it not beckon from beyond the trees —
Winking in the sunlight,
Like an old, accommodating mistress?

Now, at the turn in the road,
Seated on a gnarled bench
I spy a figure from the past.
Older than time, he is,
Wizened, broken,
His nut-brown face creased like an old shirt.
Why, I cry out in delight, it's Old Tom!
He, too, endures.
He starts to rise, extending a gnarled hand.
Young Master Derek! You've come back
After all these years!
I motion him down, his knees creaking like a
Zamobzi *zhut*, riding at anchor.

I stare into these rheumy eyes
That have seen so much
And ask the question that haunts me:
Where is my lake, Old Tom?
What has happened?
He removes the gnarled pipe from his yellow teeth,
Taps dottle from the bowl,
Croaks out an epitaph.
Gone! cries Old Tom. Gone!
Your lake is no more.
No more? My lake no more?
Oh, say not so . . .
'Tis true, the old man whispers . . .
And, as he speaks, salt tears roll down his sunken cheeks
Like freshets from a mountain stream
No more! says wise Old Tom.
It ain't a lake no more.

Meech — no longer a lake?
A cry of pain escapes me.
No longer a lake, repeats Old Tom.
No longer a lake:
Only a flawed public document.

PIERRE BERTON
KLEINBURG, ONTARIO

Meech, Rusty and the Zen of Chez Hélène

When they threw out the Friendly Giant
We should have known something was up.
Rusty is now a fricassee,
While the ghost of Jerome wanders aimlessly
In the lonely archives of the CBC.
Eerie hooves were pounding at the signing of Meech,
A logical progression from his cultural breach.
If only we had listened to the ghost of the giraffe
(Who incidentally loved Ian Tyson as much as Edith Piaf),
We would have seen it coming,
This dictum of dichotomies,
A distant dirge ringing in our ears
With a dose of American wannabe's.
If only we had listened
To the smattering of the blood of a chicken
Who is somewhere now with Louis Riel
and the spirit of Friendly
In a shaman's haven
Teaching the zen of Chez Hélène.

EDUARDO ESPEJO
TORONTO

A Senior's Income Tax Return

The message from the Taxation Centre
questions calculations
I so carefully computed.
It demands a reassessment,
mentions penalties.

I find it's their mistake,
write a carefully worded letter,
begrudging the time,
blaming their stupidity,

or
their plot for quotas
to expand government coffers,
a flim flam they figure
works well with the old,
since we're silly, having forgotten
our arithmetic, and
the batteries of our calculators
are out to lunch.

LOUISE SIMON
KINGSTON, ONTARIO

The Pirate of Ottawa

With apologies to W.S. Gilbert

He is the very model of a governmental minister
Who breaks our backs with one more tax Draconian and
    sinister,
He swears its use will not reduce the monstrous federal deficit
(I cannot use the word I'd choose — the one that starts with
    F is it).

The GST was meant to be his apogee or pinnacle,
He can't believe that it could leave us impotent and cynical,
He pays no heed to any need of all us Doubting Thomases
Who've come to see cupidity in all of Wilson's promises.

He bulls it through despite our view and then for extra
    measure he
Spends half a billion dollars from the poor depleted Treasury.
If we protest this costly mess, he swears some rosy future'll
Reduce our load way down the road and just be income-
    neutral.

If that's the plan then any man might wonder to high Heaven
    who
Would hatch a scheme that didn't cream a pile of extra
    revenue.
It's punitive and sinister, too costly to administer,
Yet he's the very model of a governmental minister!

DICK HAINSWORTH
VANCOUVER

Priorities

Oh the mail has come, joy unconfined
I'm thrilled right out of my tiny mind
For here is an envelope, big and fat
With lists inside of this and that
Books and records and tapes galore
Wait a minute there's even more
Gleaming certificates promising riches
Except of course for some minor glitches
Like failure to send this entry in
With my credit card number, check and SIN
I'll send it today, I can hardly wait
Lord knows I've got my priorities straight
For small things no longer bother me
I don't give a damn about GST.
The ozone layer will probably mend
Let polluters pollute, let Meech Lake end
Let abortionists abortion, let whales die
Let rain forests burn and the homeless cry
This superlative offer has tempered my rage
It's a Digest Sweep and I'm "Second Stage."

NOREEN OLSON
CARSTAIRS, ALBERTA

Canadian Dinner Party

We pledge to end both hunger and war.
Just eat the Earth and leave the core.

CHERRA S. RANSOM
WESTMOUNT, QUEBEC

Ode on You O Canada

As writ and recit by Yaleda Drain Farquharson, Parry Sound, Ontario, Dumb Minion Day, July 1st, 1967.

What is Canada to you?
This land so strong and true,
What does it make you think of,
And why, and where and how?
Whenever I think of my country
It seems like a great big cow.
Yes, a Guernsey or a Holsteen,
Is that sich a foolish notion?
Lappin' its fill of the waters
Of our own Pasifick Ocean.
Then chewing its cud on the Prayerees,
Rite over yer Kicking Horse Pass
In the bredbasket of our nation
As it regurgitates its grass.
And settles its mash in Ontaryo
Where its udders gently sway sweet
Waitin' fer stockbrokers to milk it,
Down there on old Bay Street.
Then to the loins of our country,
Where somethin' surely is stirrin'!
Lissen and can't you heer
A rumblin' and grumblin' and whirrin'?
The winds of change is blowin'.
Can't you hear its howls,
As we wonder at all those movements
Deep in our nation's bowels?

And so we cum to the end of the tail
Of all my little rimes...
And doesn't that always happen
To the dear old Marrytimes?
1990 Update: If yer sunuva Meechlake don't git thru, duz this
meens that Ontaryo becums Pakystand and the Marmtimes
Bangyerdesk?

DON HARRON
TORONTO

Canadian Fish-Stand Lullaby

Stand of the silver perch, home of the cleaver,
Wherefrom the fallen juice wanders as swill.
True hake from deep-sea floor,
Unprocessed albacore,
Don't can the tuna,
Don't can the tuna,
Don't can the tuna,
No.

BERNARD STEIN
DOWNSVIEW, ONTARIO

Hockey Night in Canada

I was brought up
on the sound of Foster Hewitt
announcing hockey night in Canada

Four boys and their father
Our mother and our sisters
relegated elsewhere
while we cheered for the Montreal Canadiens
or the Toronto Maple Leafs

I lost interest
by the time I was sixteen

Three cheers for those of us Canadians
who have realized that hockey's just a game
and that Canada's greatness lies in
the likes of
Norman Bethune, Emily Carr and Gabriel Dumont

Sometimes I swear
that this fair land of ours
contains
at least a dozen souls
who have seen the light

LEO GROARKE
KITCHENER, ONTARIO

60

Free Trade Election*

When I went to Jamaica the Country got sold
I knew I was missing something
I got a job, an actor's job,
so had to miss the whole thing.

I sat in Jamaica, with gange and rum
listening intently
to the sighs and the groans from so far north
to the votes as they came in.

I was in Jamaica when Bush flowered
as Maggie began her zillionth term
and oh, yes, I was there when the
Country got sold.

I felt guilty, I did,
surely there was something I could do.
Rallies, speeches, a playlet or two.
But I couldn't stomach a single one.

I'm glad I missed it, I'm glad.
I played the Duchess of Windsor in
rhinestones and paste
while the Country got sold
and Rod Steiger sat in the shade.

LINDA GRIFFITHS
TORONTO

*Linda Griffiths played the Duchess of Windsor in a television mini-series,
shot in Jamaica, about Canadian mining millionaire Sir Harry Oakes.

The Leper

I am a leper
Shunned and scorned
No welcome mat
Is out for me
Set apart from decent folk
I sit alone
And smoke, smoke, smoke

PAT HRETCHKA
GEORGETOWN, ONTARIO

Meech Ado

Une nation bilingual, oui
Avec flag avec leaf of a tree
Un red splash on white
Medicinal sight
Une bandage pour la sweet harmony

Mais regardez said flag, sur la white
Profiles glare, mouths agape avec spite
Chaque visage seems to yell
Avec voice mad as hell
L'un à l'autre to go fly a kite

NORMA OUEST LINDER
SARNIA, ONTARIO

Minimalist Nation

Felix fumed, "Two million for some paint,
When money's needed by the state?
With such a sum a wise PC
Might phone a judge, rent limos, or sell the GST."
To make some art, he placed an order:
"Canvas, two colours, ten minutes labour;
About two cowboy boots filled with blue,
And a brimming stetson of red should do."
What matter invention, reflection, proportion,
Or public policy distortion:
"To fix a divided nation,
I'll lead them to paint their frustration."
Many proved the politician's motto,
"Where fools rush in, more follow."
"We'll mass produce, auction, — better yet —
We might erase the national debt!"
Finishing, donning his hat, Felix rose,
But paint now stained *this* emperor's new clothes.
A long red neck had the blue sea parted,
And Holtmann knew more (though not much) about art than
    when he started.

STUART BROOMER
TORONTO

Tax Levy — Tee-hee

With apologies to Dennis Lee

I'm for the G.S.T.!
I'm for the G.S.T.!
If I don't get to pay it soon
I think I'll go to sea!
You can take away my pension,
You may take my R.S.P.
But please, oh please, dear Brian
Don't take the G.S.T.!

The Looney Coin's for me!
The Looney Coin's for me!
Don't take away those Loonies
From off my money tree!
You can take away John Crosbie,
You may take the trade that's free!
But I need those Loonies, Brian,
To pay my G.S.T.!

M. MONTEITH
SAUBLE BEACH, ONTARIO

The Rape of the Flock

"Patriotism is the last refuge of the scoundrel."
Samuel Johnson

What wond'rous schemes are hatched upon yon Hill,
What shallow source provides grist for the mill,
(Avowed — these lines for Atwood, Muse! are writ:
And lay no haughty claim to Papal wit)
Light is my subject, lighter still my heart,
If Pope inspire, and Muse accept my art.
What thirst for power, prithee! could incite
Such strange behaviour in a country's knight?
What grandiose delusions make him say,
He's going to bring home the B.N.A.?
Can one man to such untold heights aspire,
That he would fain invoke a nation's ire?
While war-lords slumbered gently in the West,
And only pipe dreams dared disturb their rest,
While Gallia's cousin, weary of her mate,
With je ne sais quoi decides to separate,
And those to whom this land was once well-known,
Dispute the orthograph of autochtone —
Then Caesar, rising from the royal bed,
And clutching wreath of maple to his head,
Turn'd regal eyes to greet both blushing dawn
And genuflections of his country's spawn.
But stay! The noble brow doth sudden cloud,
For in his view appears no madding crowd,
And now he knows what others long have known:
All eyes no longer turn toward the throne!

SUSAN RODOCANACHI
NEPEAN, ONTARIO

The Bird for Nova Scotia

The osprey eats our precious fish.
The sooty tern, the same.
Starlings are on which to wish
And kildeer *must* eat game.

Gulls are dupes and easy marks,
Ducks are just evaders,
Pheasants strut about in parks
And cranes are shallow waders.

Loons are a bit insane
And junkos have their habit.
Swallows are inclined to stain
And goshawks feed on rabbit.

The cowbird's morals are too loose
The blackbird tends to crow
Who's as silly as a goose?
The owls don't seem to know.

The habits of your average bird
Are quite enough to sicken
So let's support the least absurd:
Eviscerated chicken.

A. NONNY MOUSE
CHESTER BASIN

Canada Hold Your Water

O can't you see
Dear government
We should not be
In-continent!

BILL CURRY
WYNYARD, SASKATCHEWAN

Yer Hubris

Clutching his prophetic rod,
Irving Layton thinks he's God.

DENNIS LEE
TORONTO

68

Solidarity

We go out to do it
believing if everybody did a little
nobody would have to do very much.
After a while we notice
hardly anyone is doing it.
Then the behavioral psychologists hasten forward
to point out that *because* we do it
no one else does.
Does this mean if we did less
others would do more?
Or that if nobody did it
everybody would do it?
Since we lack proof the latter is true, however,
we go out and do it.

TOM WAYMAN
WINLAW, BRITISH COLUMBIA

Mission: Impossible

Why don't the homeless just go home, Joe Clark should get a chin.
Illiterates should learn to read, You drop-outs, drop back in.
Somebody should do something about this greenhouse effect.
And women should be treated equally and shown respect.
Why don't the unemployed get jobs? You doctors should cure AIDS.
"I'm tired," single moms complain. Why don't they hire maids?
And if your kids don't like you, buy them stuff until they do.
If you're too fat, stop eating. If you do drugs, stop that too.
All politicians should tell the whole truth and nothing but.
And finally, those with nothing to say, keep your mouths shut.

JOANNE BRIGDON
BRAMALEA, ONTARIO

What Was His Loco Motive?

He stopped us in our tracks, but we must admit we gambled
By electing a Prime Minister named Brain . . . (just slightly
    scrambled).
He spoke about reductions, but therein lies the dichotomy —
We didn't just get Via "cuts" — we got a trackiotomy!
A woman's right to choo-choos was but part of the debate;
To plea for ties that bind was just to rail — against cruel fate.
As the trains pulled out, we called: "Come back sometime and
    see us!"
And slowly waving, sobbed: "Farewell . . . Adieu . . . Via con Dios!"

DEBORAH LEE
VANCOUVER

Of Brian and Ronnie and Free Trade

How wonderful his breath must smell
From his bid to be famous
He sold our nation straight to hell
And kissed old Ronnie's anus

SCOTT PIATKOWSKI
OTTAWA

The Average Canadian

there's this guy at the free concert who looks familiar   nice tie
good shoes gravelly low voice seductive   and he has a way
with words

THE AVERAGE CANADIAN he says talking to this friend
of his mike someone in
the v.i.p. row (oh and barbara's here and peter! peter and
wendy my god)

but the music's started and this mike guy is shaking his head
in awe as the
strings soar up and up! an explosion of clapping yes! it *must*
be good! for
once no question   he's grinning in relief clapping lookin at . . .
brian

for yes   that's who it is: my prime minister himself telling
anyone who
will listen that THE AVERAGE CANADIAN WANTS TO
BE PART OF THE DECISION-
MAKING PROCESS AND THAT'S WHY YOU AND YOU AND YOU
TOO GET TO PAY THE SAME
TAX   THE SAME TAX AS ANY MISERABLE CRUDDY OLD
MILLIONAIRE   so there

and now the strings are at it again the air thick with voices
joining in
a coloratura soprano swinging easily into some jazz that
obnoxious little
hot dog of a tenor trying to outshine everyone else the music
climaxing
and mike mouthing to brian oh mull! isn't this somethin? *how*
do they do
it mull   you are the wind beneath my wings   oh mull

mull's standing now   waving at the people   smiling in
    shocked recognition
as he points into their midst   THE AVERAGE CANADIAN
    he lets out once more
feet apart relaxed you are the wings beneath my wind
HALLELUJAH!

mike weeps openly

RUTH KRAHN
EDMONTON

There Was an Old Pol

There was an old pol from Victoria
Who spent his time chanting Gloria.
    When they said Vander Zalm
    Don't you give a small dalm
For the forests, his language grew gorier.

GEORGE WOODCOCK
VANCOUVER

Basic Black: A Con-trite Reflection

I warrant I've never come upon
a twit as pompous as our Con
He's only human, so God knows
We'll pardon him — but not his prose

CHARLES MACLI
TORONTO

74

To _ _ _ _ _ _ _ _ _ _

Egomaniac, loud and wild,
Admired by many you've reviled;
Hurling (you're Jove on Mount Olympus)
Vulgar epithets upon us;
Scratch you and you do orate
In authentic Billingsgate;
Though a poet by profession,
You're untrammeled by discretion;
You have your bardic tongue disgraced
By such utter lack of taste;
I nominate you, hat in hand,
Poet Laureate of Chutzpah-land!

IRVING LONDON
WESTMOUNT, QUEBEC

Once Upon a Time, My Dear

Once upon a time, my dear,
I loved you very much.
I hung upon your every word
And trembled at your touch.

But that was quite some time ago
Before you fell from grace
And now some other silly fool
Has come to take your place.

DOROTHY MICHAELL
SCARBOROUGH, ONTARIO

Can__da 2002

As soon as he'd seen us the reporter from Venus
Filed this story he sent to his boss:

"They have trade that is free but they pay G.S.T.
And they're running the place at a loss.

There's another great riddle, there's a hole in the middle
And the country is broken in two.

There are senators (old) and the truth can be told,
They seem to have nothing to do.

There are tribes from the West who claim they're the best
And Easterners preening with pride.

There are Newfies who screech when they think about Meech
And the Prairies along for the ride.

A delicate slap caused a terrible flap
And a media circus one night.

The fat lady swung both her fist and her tongue
It seems that her dress was too tight.

I suggest you persuade those who want to invade
That this Can__da is simply bad news.

There are just some tree stumps and big Ottawa dumps
Of collections of used Gucci shoes."

S.Y. RICHARDSON
WEST VANCOUVER

The Black Forest

Inspired by the alleged statement of Liberal Welfare Minister
Black that children were B.C.'s second-most valuable resource,
after lands and forests.

I think I shall never see
A child as lovely as a tree.
However parenthood be planned,
No child can match productive land.
A child just sits and costs all day,
But trees lift leafy arms and pay.
A child with hungry mouth and eye
Makes saving difficult; we try
To draw a line between devotion
And rather over-priced emotion
As firmly as we can — alack;
The future may indeed be Black.
I gladly rank a son or daughter
Ahead of coal or fish or water
But valuewise, a child, of course,
Is just our second-best resource.

DAVE BARRETT
DEWDNEY

Grieve la Difference

Peace and order aren't so bad
(Good government we never had)
While they get Liberty —
(Life too!)
And all the Joy they can pursue.

C'est ne pas faire:
Yanks have all three,
Plus cheaper food
Porn on TV
Discounted stoves
High style for less
Fresher loaves
A flag they bless...

No! Here I Stand, in gabardine!*

*Until I get that card of green.

ALLAN GOULD
TORONTO

Modern Man

Once he had the tallest tower on the block
but he was the first to subscribe to cable.
When he goes for a beer with the guys after work
he asks whether the bar has a good television.
"Gotta be informed," he says.
He was an early convert to pay TV —
carefully savouring the saving in movie costs,
though they had never gone much to the movies.
When pay TV proved disappointing,
he borrowed money
to buy a satellite dish.
Now he can get 58 channels and
he reads *TV Guide* like a daily devotional.
His best friend died last week.
He didn't get to the funeral.
CBC was airing a special on "Loving and Sharing."
The times conflicted.

JOAN EYOLFSON CADHAM
STE ANNE DE BELLEVUE, QUEBEC

Showdown

A gunslinger, name of Pierre,
With an ego quite extraordinaire,
Came to harangue
The Meech Lake gang
With a finger thrust high in the air!

LAWRENCE ALLEN WILSON
PENTICTON, BRITISH COLUMBIA

And Then There Were None

Eleven first ministers, sitting on a beach,
Writing constitutions by a lake named Meech.

Eleven first ministers, handing 'round a pen,
One didn't ratify and then there were ten.

Ten first ministers, standing in a line,
An election was lost, and then there were nine.

Nine first ministers paralleled too late,
One called: "Rescind!" and then there were eight.

Eight first ministers knew not what to do,
Dallied and dawdled until there were two.

Two first ministers knew the game was done,
Ottawa gave up, and then there was one.

One *premier minister* with no place in the sun,
And so he separated —

— and then there were none!

WILLIAM A. EDMISTON
PIERREFONDS, QUEBEC

B.C. at Night

Upon Minister of Health Peter Dueck's celibacy-advocation
approach to the AIDS problem.

All over B.C. in the still of the night
Husbands lean over to turn out the light.
Is she really asleep? he gives her a poke,
Whispers what Dueck's ordained for married folk.

And as she rolls over from one side t'other
He silently swears — more love comes from Rover.
He lies on his back, he stares at the moon,
and he wonders what Peter Dueck is doin'.

Again — she rolls over — and says with a sigh,
"What's good for the Duecks is not good for I.
All day, I wash, I clean, and I bake,
I want to sleep now, I have a headache."

Now, all you restive folk, as yet unwed,
Listen this once, ere you jump into bed,
You may ignore Peter Dueck,
You may disobey God,
But, you'll not escape the B.C. monogamy squad.

PATRICIA McCREERY
VANCOUVER

A Mare Usque ad Nauseam

From coast to coast take up the fight
While time is left uphold the right
Pour bitter venom from your heart
Lest Canada should fall apart.

We'll not prevent these racist spats
With mounties wearing "proper" hats
Instead each petty bias bring
As we unite to do our thing
Forget all senseless self-restraint
And loudly voice each vile complaint

"The Frenchies all can have Quebec
No one speaks white there, what the heck."

"Who cares how those dumb Newfies vote
We'll set the jokers all afloat."

"Those trouble-makers in the west
Don't care if we all get depressed."

Let all us "frogs" and "têtes carrés"
Just get together for one day
And we can reconfederate
United in communal hate.

HUGH MACDONALD
MONTAGUE, PRINCE EDWARD ISLAND

Life Is Fair

One day I met up with a man on a street who told me
that life was fair
He wore a grey suit with pin stripes of silver that matched
the pin stripes in his hair
He was bigger than me, and I never did see his face
but I didn't care
The thing I remember the most about him was he told me
that life was fair

And a decade before with crossed legs on the floor
I studied my favourite cartoon
A flaxen-haired princess adorned by her prince
turns to black silhouette by the moon
And then it would end when they mounted the friendly and
"ready to fly away" mare
I remember the colour and warmth and the moment
they told me that life was fair

You strange silly person, dealing with life because
"nobody said it was fair"
They did, yes they did, 21 trillion times
And each time that they did, I was there

KATHRYN GREENWOOD
LONDON, ONTARIO

Clearcut Promises

Old forests soared centuries high
'Til Mac Blo came with chain saws.
Alas the promises they make
Are camouflage for what they take
Leaving clearcuts in their wake:
"FORESTS FOREVER" . . . GONE.

GERTRUDE LAWRIE
SIDNEY, NOVA SCOTIA

Hymn — or Her — to a Good Ol' Boy

How sweet the name John Crosbie sounds
In every woman's ear
It gives us goosebumps just to know
The jolly lad is near

For he can mouth his ignorance
With jokes both cruel and crude
While a girl must learn to spread her legs,
Be flattered by glances lewd

Our native peoples, gays and all
the handicapped, what's more
Are not supposed to carp and whine
And say they're feeling sore

So, John, let's hope you're feeling good
About your dirty words
"But Oi really meant no harm you know
To you silly little birds!"

PATRICIA BLACK
LONDON, ONTARIO

Canadian Roulette

Let's not invent any more weapons.
Let's grope in the fog
wearing coarse wool underwear instead.
Let's be kind to one another
and let's not write any more hate poetry.

Let's pretend we're in love with one another.
You go first.

SUSAN MUSGRAVE
SIDNEY, BRITISH COLUMBIA

Back Bacon and Beer

It sizzles on the frying pan;
I love the sound I hear;
I smile at all the bubbles,
— then I add a splash o' beer.

I lick my lips and marvel
As it turns a granite hue.
I flip the beggars over, and
— I tip another brew.

They're done! I lift them from the pan,
Then, gently, as I do,
I lay another panful, and
— I tip another brew.

Yeah, there's nothin' I can think of
That can stir a northern heart,
Like beer and greasy bacon, but. . .
— it really makes you fart.

DON CAMERON
KENORA, ONTARIO

The Jet

There once was a Golden Jet
Who had a young son named Brett
His hair fell away
Now he wears a toupee
While his son blasts the puck in the net.

ROYDON STRANK
OAKVILLE, ONTARIO

Owed t'Brian

stucco white pan o milk
and anemic too.
like wet lard on pan dandy
like flour filled blank candy
the simple servants move blandly.
to the sounds of the
bulimic heavers on the hill.
who grow ill with portions of
undigested peach flake and brie charade,
freshly passed on the wall.
the prime regurgitator oversees all.
and
he stands small.

JOHN SKWAROK
OTTAWA

Confederation, eh?

What was Confederation, Dad?
Came the question from the son.
There was a time, my boy, you see
When Canada was one.
A mighty nation, shore to shore,
United in its glory,
Ten provinces, the Yukon,
And the Northwest Territories.
But the U.S. needed fresh supplies
And soon we got "Free Trade."
We lost our trees, our fish, our jobs,
A mistake, we knew, we'd made.
Then trains were cut out to the West,
And B.C. soon withdrew.
Quebec was told "Forget the French,"
So they, too, said "Adieu!"
The Maritimes, without a link,
Soon had their fate decided,
They joined the States, and that, my son
Is how we were divided.

BARBARA J. STRUDWICK
KAMLOOPS, BRITISH COLUMBIA

Politics

it's a cold, cold basic formula in Canada:
politician = gangster
should be scrawled in white chalk on a slate grey sky
because it's a lesson everybody ought to learn
though the animals will deny it
shark membrane eyes closing from the bottom upward
to protect them as they shake their heads
the better to saw the meat off your bones
tax money just a gravity feed
(like piss)
disappearing in fast wet connections down
porcelain damp, ammonia scent, tarnished brass, copper green
mystery holes
as secret as what happens to the bodies of birds when
they die in the city
any truth unexpected
like the sound made by a snowflake
hitting your ear.

BARRY HAMMOND
EDMONTON

Adultery in the Safeway

i see him in the tomatoes   impressed that he is letting the
vegetables/fruits fall onto the cart ribs bare enjoy making
breath noises with my back to him try to horn him up a bit
by the organic tomatilloes   we pass the freshly squeezed
grapefruits   take turns sampling crackers surrounded by fake
cheese and red wrapped goudas   he asks me what's breakfast
yoghurt   not catching on i explain fat content   he has
snapped off the lid of a small olympia black cherry dipping
his finger in offers me some my tongue must jump to catch the
purple pieces of sweetness   the carton our mouths his fingers
our tongues are everywhere   the butcher nowhere late late
sunday night   smells of masking tape and orange juice freezer
blueberry milkiness and i've just come for noodles

MARTHA HILLHOUSE
VANCOUVER

A Surfeit of Democracy

Out here in B.C. we've no patience
With logic in government men.
What we buy is the smile and the sound bite.
What we get is a middle-aged Ken.

Now the school system's caught Zalm's attention.
(His own schooling's just an addendum.)
He's decided that funding's a matter
For decision by our referendum.

See, about public schools: of all voters,
Just one third have kids who attendum.
It's election time soon and he's saying
We'll cut taxes with this referendum.

When school kids were coming in hungry
He said that their parents should tendum.
The poor are too costly. Let's ban them.
Put that on the next referendum!

They're our hard-earned bucks, so why don't we
Hold votes every time that they spendum.
Me first! Up with bottom-line thinking!
Vote for Zalm and his dear referendumb.

JANE BARKER WRIGHT
VANCOUVER

The Secretary

What the well-dressed girl will wear:

Wash'n'wear polyester chalk-stripe wrap-around in slimming
come-again navy blue. Sixteen ridiculous dollars. Designed
to please the man who calls her "Secretary Girl."

Cute little navy blue pumps with high heels high enough to
    entice,
low enough to run. Armé de Salvation. $4. But only her
best friend needs to know.

This snappy ensemble is completed by a fin-blue cotton
    t-shirt
with slit-neck and droopy loopy sleeves by Alfred Sung. One
hundred and twenty-five dollars. She was depressed and
    she . . .
simply had to go shopping.

Nevertheless.
She stands.
A veritable soldierette,
On the very brink of pay equity.
Success will be hers before you can go:
"Phhht! Phhht!"

TOMSON HIGHWAY
TORONTO

Pope! Thou Should'st Be Living at This Hour.

Know then thyself, presume not God to scan;
The proper study of mankind is man...
Fix'd like a plant on his peculiar spot,
To draw nutrition, propagate, and rot.
Alexander Pope
Essay on Man (1734)

Of Canada I sing, a branchy plant
Ungovernable and irrelevant.
Servant of empire once, today we're free
To disagree on what we're free to be.
A century and more of introspection's
Turned up few Canadian connections —
Except a southside itch to imitate
That marks us as an imitation state.
Seeking identity in what you are
And where you are is circular —
Like trying to find the light-switch in the dark
By turning on the light: it will not work.

In this predicament the thing to do
Is reinvent oneself each year or two —
With constitutional repatriation,
Accords named after lakes, and immigration.
What's needed is a federal apparatus
To make all equal but with special status;
Business free but underwritten; art
Part of the mainstream but apart;
Education free for all, awarded
To applicants whose parents can afford it;
Last, a constitution with a clause
Exempting those who choose to flout its laws.

Since no such nation ever was or could be,
Whatever makes us think that this one should be?

MAVOR MOORE
VANCOUVER

95

Ontario's Main Street

Remember he who sang with glee,
"Oh, who would o'er the Downs with me?"
Our Downs are getting hard to see —
Beside the Four-Oh-One.

Each time we visit Blue-Jay-Dum
We risk a trip to Kingdom-Come;
Get in the other lane, old son —
You're on the Four-Oh-One.

From Tee-Oh through to London Town
Don't let the traffic get you down.
Good grief, we almost hit that clown —
Here on the Four-Oh-One.

Development just grows and grows —
The farmland merely goes and goes —
And still the semi goes and goes
Along the Four-Oh-One.

Our country goes from sea to sea —
And who would like to ride with me —
And be Canadian, strong and free —
Here on the Four-Oh-One?

JOAN GLOVER SMITH
STRATFORD, ONTARIO

The Perfect Apple

If you will serve me,
said the devil to the saint,
you may eat this perfect apple.
No ugly scab mars this apple;
we have chemicals for scab.
No worm; we have worm chemicals,
and shape and shine and size chemicals,
and one that lets you keep it 6 months in the fridge
because bacteria cannot survive in this apple.

Sounds OK, said the saint,
In what way would I serve you?

In a little way, said the devil,
With the life of just one child in 3,000.

Take your perfect apple to Hell,
said the saint, but answer one question:
Isn't apple-offering the snake's job?

Well . . . ah . . . traditionally . . . ah,
we have a little problem;
chemicals killed the snake.

GERALD HARRIS
VICTORIA

The Law of Averages

He's your average politician and he likes to say his mission
Is to serve the worthy voters of his riding,
While the other party's candidate is second place and second rate
And thoroughly deserves a damn good hiding.

Our friend is glad to promise more (to help us—that's what
    friends are for)
With money gathered in a manner painless
From someone rich who lives elsewhere (they've got the
    bucks, it's only fair)
And those who'd snub free money must be brainless.

With tireless repetition he presents his timely vision
Of the role that fate has chosen him to play.
If we'll grant him public office (down the hall from where the
    trough is)
He'll ensure the sun will rise and set each day.

But you and I, we know the score — he's just another
    pompous bore
Who likes to talk on issues quite confusing
Don't bug me with that heavy stuff, I pay my taxes, that's
    enough,
Change channels — let's find something more amusing.

'Cause I'm just your average voter and there's nothing much
    remoter
Than the chance I'll make a difference to his show,
So I'll stay home on voting day — he'll win the game but I
    won't play —
Who lets these bozos win I'll never know!

JAMES R. BIGSBY
VICTORIA

Ballade of the Boondocks

I spent a day in Dogwood Creek —
at least I think it was a day
although it felt more like a week.
I thought I'd never get away.
They showed me cows and calves and hay.
I walked until my knees were weak.
Forgive me twitching when I say
I spent a day in Dogwood Creek.

The tea they brought was far from weak,
a sort of liquid orange clay,
but when I went to take a leak
before the outhouse grim and grey
were cattle that had gone astray
and somewhat in a state of pique.
My bladder still recalls the way
I spent a day in Dogwood Creek.

Some think that there is a mystique
in far off places like Malay
or Madagascar and they seek
the rites of Rohini and Re.
Myself, I never mean to lay
my head on Mars or Martinique.
I've had my fill of disarray.
I spent a day in Dogwood Creek.

Envoi

Prince, hold the hellfire and unsay
that sentence; you've no need to wreak
your judgement or to burn and flay:
I spent a day in Dogwood Creek.

ROBIN SKELTON
VICTORIA

Mulroney and Wilson

Mulroney and Wilson are mooches,
they treat us no better than pooches.
My post-tax pay handles
the thinnest of sandals
While Brian pads 'round in his Gooches

GARY KATZ
TORONTO

Sunday Breakfast

He brought my Sunday breakfast to bed,
He indulged my most whimsical wishes,
He used every pot and pan in the house —
Now *I* must wash the dishes!

LOIS R. KERR
VANCOUVER

Applause

A man from the government bureau
came to speak to the Indian tribe.
"We'll build you new roads and new fences."
"Hoya! Hoya!" the natives replied.
Encouraged, the clerk was expansive,
"New buildings, a post office, too."
In proportion to each promise added,
the volume of "Hoya" cries grew.
Reluctant to leave this reception
he lingered to see the reserve;
his gaze fell on a large bull pen
which instantly summoned his nerve.
"Would you mind if I step through the gateway?
It's uncommon to see bulls well-bred."
The chieftain agreed, but with caution,
"Don't step in the hoya," he said.

HAZEL CAMPBELL TOMLINSON
THUNDER BAY, ONTARIO

The Waist Land

I   A Game of Gin

April is our slowest month
Nothing but gin-rummy for idle hands
Or standing by the cash register
Watching St Paul Street through the glass
Over the pinned backs of lacquer-headed mannequins.
Summer revives us, bringing high-school girls
Turning the corridor into the dressing room
With fluorescent light showing
Blotchy faces to the looking-glass
Above twisted straps and decaying nylon underwear.

A little game in the back of the store:
"Are you in or out, Harry?" "Listen, I'm
Losing my shirt." "Never mind your shirt.
Harry, are you in or out?"

We play in the back of the store
And go south in the winter.

II   The Burial of the Dead

"Did I get a shock on Spadina Avenue today —"
"Jack, I don't want to hear about it!"
"And him just back from Miami —"
"Jack, I don't want to know!"
"I only saw him a week ago
the picture of health."

III   What the Auditor Said

The chair he sat in, a Bauhaus reject
With cigarette scars on foam-rubber
Facing the old canal.
"I ask you, Lou, who needs it?
Am I looking for a coronary?"
Slowly, starting maybe in the rack
Reserved for house dresses
The business quietly got up, backed to the door
Smiled apologetically, and left.

Shmate, shmate, shmate.

HOWARD ENGEL
TORONTO

Gretzky

A sportsman from Edmonton said:
"'To see hockey I'd rise from the dead!
But when Gretzky was traded,
my interest soon faded.
And now I watch baseball instead!"

GRAEME STEWART
DARTMOUTH, NOVA SCOTIA

Ode to Readers of *This Mag*

A drowsy smugness fills my head
As though in *This Mag* I had read
Of sins and greed of Grit and Tory
Of Wafflers in their futile glory
Of unions smashed, strikers betrayed
Of Luddite theories on Free Trade
Of global crimes by Yanqui hands
Of Canucks stealing tribal lands

And as Stan Persky takes brave aim
At tough targets like Vander Zalm
And every profit's deemed obscene
By Watkins, Saul, Atwood, and Crean
I dream I am a man of action
To rise above the armchair faction
But lest this dream go to my head
I'd best renew my sub instead.

ROBERT CARROLL
EDMONTON

HELP STAMP OUT
MEN'S WHITE PATENT
LEATHER SHOES!!!
SUBSCRIBE...

Ode to a Gentle Lake

I know two things about "LAC MEECH,"
It hath both water and a beach;
But let's BEWARE; t'would be a SIN
If our GREAT COUNTRY drowned therein!

Said poor LAC MEECH: "It is a shame
Those Feds have so abused my name!
I am a quiet and humble chap
With NO ambitions on the map
And NO desire to air my views
In public on the daily news...
I think I'll seek my friends the Trout
To pull the plug and let me out!
And then I'll be in no more trouble,
I'll sink downhill in one big bubble;
Whilst all you lakes of GATINEAU
Will fight to take my place I know!

I know two things about MEECH LAKE,
T'was fun to swim around and bake
Upon his shores. Now down the hill
Come children, you may find him still!

JOAN RYS
HUDSON, QUEBEC

105

Galluping from Democracy

Nineteen times out of twenty
This poll is accurate to plus or minus one per cent.
Nineteen times out of twenty
This represents the opinion of Canadians
(Allowing for sampling error).
Nineteen times out of twenty
The people interviewed had
Too little knowledge of the subject.
Nineteen times out of twenty
The clients trust the survey.
If it suits them!
That's POLL-ITICS.

RICHARD HATFIELD
FREDERICTON, NEW BRUNSWICK

But, being summer, virtually all Canadians did agree that, given the choice between submitting to yet another one of these polls and making out in the back of a customized 1957 Chevy,...

Sh! It's Time for the News

Are you really interested in saving Canada
  from the indistinct Meech Lake Accord?

Does your heart long to slay the dragon
  of racial or aboriginal discord?

Do you give a damn about bilingualism,
  or the Bank of Canada lowering interest rates?

Do you worry about daggers in Mounties turbans,
  or that too many females are getting raped by their dates?

Is the perpetrator of the GST a real curmudgeon?
  Does thinking of his boss put you in high dudgeon?

Could fretting about Free Trade give you a pain in the derrière?
  Would you shed crocodile tears over jobs that aren't there?

Are drugs, guns, and liquor behind all of our troubles?
  Has child-molestation more than tripled, not doubled?

Are rent-gouging landlords demanding still more cash?
  Do violence, gangs, and crime go from bash to smash?

Are breadlines getting longer, the number of homeless increasing?
  Will pollution and acid rain continue without ceasing?

After listening to all these disasters, what can one do or say
  when some idiotic broadcaster signs off with "HAVE A
  GOOD DAY!!!"

FLORENCE E. BRODIE
TORONTO

Oh! Canada

We're just a couple of regular guys
Canadian boys are we.
Hockey is the game we love,
We watch it on T.V.

We're two of Canada's finest
Who enjoy a hearty chat.
A beer or two can't hurt you
There's no denyin' that.

We like to watch our Canadian sport
On the tube behind the bar,
And occasionally when things get rough
We go a little far.

So when Gretzky elbowed Messier
My buddy hit the roof,
He also broke the T.V.
The Mother-huggin' goof.

He slugged the guy beside him
And now we're all in jail
A living testimonial
To hockey and stout ale.

JOHN MARGERM
TORONTO

Oh Canada

Oh Canada,
Our home and native land.
True patriarch hearts,
At Washington's command.
With glowering hearts
We see thee razed,
The "True North" going for free.
So step on me, Oh Ottawa,
My country's gone P.C.
"God," weeps the land,
"No trade is free."
Oh Canada, I'll say a prayer for thee!
Oh Canada, I'll say a prayer for thee!

ROGER MUSSELMAN
TORONTO

VIA Con Dios

I'm getting nervous;
What are you doing with that
Last spike, anyway?

GLEN STONE AND DENIS WOOLLINGS
TORONTO

Ode to Barbed Lyres et al.

I will take up my lyre
and sing you a lie
but your mind will not know it,
you will not reason why,
for my song will enchant you
and reason will die
while I gild the white lily
and barb the white lie.

Hence, though neither a barber
nor liar I be,
take not my good lyre
nor my lying from me
but accept them with pleasure
and sing them all three,
my lovely barbed lyre,
my lying — and me.

ELISE GOLDSMITH
TORONTO

ACKNOWLEDGMENTS

Thanks above all to Ellen Vanstone, who co-ordinated the Barbed Lyres contest for *This Magazine*, and who edited the text along with *This Magazine*. Special thanks to Margaret Atwood for the idea; to Margaret Atwood, Allan Fotheringham and Nancy White for arduous service as judges; and to Terry Mosher, a.k.a. Aislin. Thanks as well to "Morningside," *Saturday Night, Books in Canada, Quill and Quire, Frank* and Key Porter. Thanks finally to all those Canadians from every part of the country who contributed their humour and anger in verse form.

THE EDITORS
THIS MAGAZINE

ILLUSTRATION CREDITS

The cartoon on page 60 was first published in *Maclean's*. The cartoons on pages 2, 19, 20, 22, 31, 39, 44, 62, 63, 71, 85, 86, 95, 101 and 106 were first published in the *Montreal Gazette*. The cartoon on page 41 was first published in *Today* magazine; the cartoon on page 32 in *Toronto Life*; and the cartoon on page 82 in the *Toronto Star*. All cartoons were supplied by Aislin.